EXPLORING WOOD

AND THE FOREST

By Jean Warren

Illustrations by Gary Mohrmann

Warren Publishing House, Inc.
Everett, Washington

Some of the activity ideas in this book were originally contributed by *Totline Newsletter* subscribers. We wish to acknowledge:

Betty Ruth Baker, Waco, TX; Julie Bakerlis, Dudley, MA; Janice Bodenstedt, Jackson, MI; DeeDee Crocket, Marchfield, WI; Marlene Filsinger, Snyder, NY; Peggy Hanley, St. Joseph, MI; Mary Haynes, Lansing, MI; Nancy J. Heimark, Grand Forks, ND; Erma Hunt, Winston-Salem, NC; Ellen Javernick, Loveland, CO; Debbie MacMillan, Wayne, NJ; Susan M. Paprocki, Northbrook, IL; Susan Peters, Upland, CA; Jane Roake, Oswego, IL; Betty Silkunas, Lansdale, PA; Kathy Sizer, Tustin, CA; Jacki Smallwood, Royersford, PA; Diane Thom, Maple Valley, WA; Becky Valenick, Rockford, IL; Bonnie Woodard, Shreveport, LA.

Editorial Staff:
    Editorial Manager: Kathleen Cubley
    Editor: Elizabeth McKinnon
    Contributing Editor: Gayle Bittinger
    Copy Editor: Brenda Mann Harrison
    Proofreader: Kris Fulsaas
    Editorial Assistant: Erica West

Design and Production Staff:
    Art Manager: Jill Lustig
    Book Design/Layout: Sarah Ness
    Cover: Eric Stovall
    Production Manager: JoAnna Brock

ISBN 0-911019-60-X

Library of Congress Catalog Card Number 92-62464
Printed in the United States of America
Published by: Warren Publishing House, Inc.
        P.O. Box 2250
        Everett, WA 98203

20 19 18 17 16 15 14 13 12 11 10 9 8 7 6 5 4 3

INTRODUCTION

As with all Totline books, it is the goal of the Exploring Series to provide parents and teachers with creative activity suggestions that are appropriate for young children. These activities are designed to build on children's natural curiosity and interests and serve as stepping stones to additional learning discoveries.

Exploring Wood begins with a chapter on carpentry that offers a variety of woodworking activities and includes suggestions for setting up a simple, safe carpentry area. Working with wood provides opportunities for children to develop fine and gross motor skills plus eye-hand coordination. Also, it lets children solve problems and be creative, thus building self-esteem.

The second chapter of *Exploring Wood* provides an around-the-curriculum exploration of trees. Included are activity suggestions for art, science, language, learning games, movement, music, social studies and snacks. You and your children can decide how far you want to go with these activities. If there is interest, you may wish to lead your children into a total-environment unit about the forest.

Activities dealing with the North American forest, forest animals and forest preservation are provided in the final chapters of *Exploring Wood*. If you work with older children and want to expand learning, a natural extension would be a unit on the rain forest and the importance of preserving it.

Exploring Wood ends with a set of forest animal patterns that can be copied and used for various learning activities, plus a list of children's books about wood and the forest.

I wish you and your children *bon chance* as you begin your explorations. I hope you will find the world of wood and the forest environment as fascinating as I do.

Jean Warren

CONTENTS

Forest Preservation

Forest Patterns

Children's Book List

Carpentry Fun

Carpentry Area

Work Space — Make sure that your carpentry area is spacious and situated away from other play areas. A separated area inside or outside your building would be ideal.

Workbench — Provide a workbench that is low enough for your children to bend over when they are hammering or sawing. Make sure that it has one end that can hold a clamp. Try a wooden cable spool, a sturdy wooden box or an old table cut down to size.

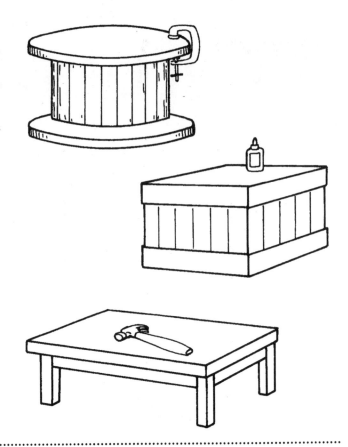

Carpentry Supplies

Scrap Wood — Look for wood (preferably softwood) to use for your children's carpentry projects. For example, check grocery stores for wooden boxes, lumber yards or construction sites for piles of free wood scraps, or Christmas tree farms for pieces of bark and sections of tree trunks.

Other Woodworking Supplies — Include in your carpentry area materials such as these: different grades of sandpaper, nails with large heads, different kinds of large screws, wood glue, bottle caps, fabric pieces, wooden beads and plastic shapes.

Suggested Tools

Purchase real tools in small sizes from a hardware store. Suggested tools include those that follow.

- claw hammer
- ball-peen hammer
- coping saw
- hand saw
- ordinary screwdriver
- Phillips screwdriver
- hand drill
- pliers
- rasp
- C-clamps
- ruler
- T-square
- safety goggles

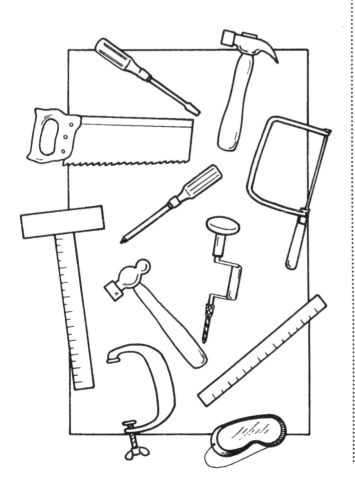

Tool Tips

Tool Storage — Trace the shapes of your tools onto a piece of pegboard. Add appropriate hooks and label each tracing. Attach the pegboard to a wall at your children's eye level. Encourage the children to hang the tools in their proper places after each use.

Tool Safety — Show your children how to use and care for each of your carpentry tools. Set out examples of real and toy tools and discuss the differences. Have your children sort the tools into two groups. Ask questions such as these: "How can you tell that this is a toy hammer, not a real one? What might happen if you used a real saw when you were playing a game?"

Storage and Clean-up Tips

■ Provide a separate storage bin for each kind of material used in the carpentry area.

■ After a child finishes working in the carpentry area, have him or her return all tools to their proper places and all materials to their proper bins.

■ Provide your children with a small broom and a dustpan for cleaning the floor of the carpentry area.

■ Keep a large magnet handy. Let your children move it over the carpentry area to collect stray nails and screws. (*Note:* The magnet will not attract nails or screws that are made of aluminum.)

Carpentry Safety Tips

■ Limit the number of children that can work at the bench at one time.

■ Make sure your children wear safety goggles at all times in the carpentry area.

■ Remind your children to use the correct tool for the job.

■ Have your children use C-clamps instead of their hands to hold boards for hammering or sawing.

■ Remind your children to keep tools only in the carpentry area.

■ Have your children properly put away all tools after each use.

■ Be sure to have adult supervision in the carpentry area whenever children are working.

■ Keep all tools in good condition.

■ Remind your children not to hammer, saw, or drill into the workbench.

■ Do not allow children to put nails, screws or other carpentry materials into their mouths.

Age-Appropriate Activities

■ Children should be at least 3 years old before they are allowed into the carpentry area. Be sure to adapt all woodworking activities to fit the individual needs of your children.

■ Three-year-olds will enjoy the process of sanding, hammering, sawing, etc., rather than actually building things. Provide your children with many opportunities for mastering these carpentry skills.

■ Four-year-olds will gradually begin to enjoy gluing or nailing pieces of wood together. As they gain experience, encourage them to create their own masterpieces, using scrap materials provided in the carpentry area.

■ For all ages, woodworking provides opportunities for problem solving. Problems can range from "How high can I stack this wood?" to "Which nail works best?" to "What can I put on my car to make wheels?" Encourage your children to experiment when seeking solutions.

■ All ages can participate in field trips to lumber yards, tree farms, etc., to find scrap wood. Give your children paper bags with their names on them for bringing back wood pieces.

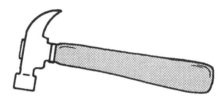

Helpful Carpentry Hints

■ When introducing tools to your children, begin with the hammer. It is the easiest tool for young children to manipulate.

■ Introduce sawing last. It is the most dangerous and difficult carpentry skill to master.

■ Have adequate tools and carpentry materials for everyone.

■ Encourage your children to help one another while they are working.

■ If your children become too stressed or tired while working in the carpentry area, offer to set aside projects so that they can be finished at a later time.

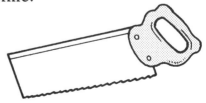

Hammering

Hammering Fun — For beginning hammering, let your children pound large-headed nails into an old tree stump or a log placed in your carpentry area. Or let them hammer nails or golf tees into large chunks of plastic foam.

Bottle Cap Fun — Let your children use hammers to flatten bottle caps on a block of wood. Later, the caps can be nailed in stacks of three to the ends of narrow pieces of wood to make rhythm instruments.

Nail Pictures — For older children, draw shapes, such as triangles or stars, on wooden boards. Have the children hammer nails into the shape outlines to make nail pictures. Or draw large numerals or alphabet letters on the boards.

Sanding

Sanding Fun — Set out sandpaper of different grades, ranging from coarse to extra-fine. Also set out a variety of small wood pieces. Let your children experiment with sanding the wood. As they work, encourage them to tell how the wood changes.

Building Blocks — Obtain wood block scraps from a lumber yard or a construction site. Let your children sand and paint the wood scraps to make an extra set of building blocks for your block area.

Sandpaper Blocks — Give each child two small blocks of wood. Have the children sand their blocks until they are smooth. Then have them glue sandpaper squares to one side of their blocks and wooden spool "handles" to the opposite side. When the glue has dried, let your children use their sandpaper blocks as rhythm instruments at music time.

Carpentry Fun

Inserting Screws

Simple Screw Fun — To help a child learn how to insert a screw into wood, try this. First, have the child hammer a nail partway into a block of softwood and then wiggle it out. Next, have the child rub the end of a screw on a bar of soap and then screw it with a screwdriver into the nail hole. Let the child practice screwing and unscrewing the screw.

Which Screwdriver? — Screw various kinds and sizes of screws (including Phillips screws) into a piece of two-by-four. Set out a variety of screwdrivers (including one or more Phillips screwdrivers). Let one child at a time experiment with finding out which screwdriver works the best on each screw.

Key Holders — Let older children make simple key holders. Have your children sand narrow pieces of wood, approximately 12 inches long. Next, have each child screw in four cup hooks across the front of his or her wood piece. Then have the child insert two screw eyes into the top of the wood piece for hanging. If desired, let the children decorate their key holders with paint, decals or stickers.

Gluing

Gluing Fun — Provide each child with a square piece of flat wood. Set out glue, brushes and pieces of scrap wood. Let your children glue the scrap wood to their wood squares to make houses, towers or free-form structures.

Craft-Stick Shapes — Let your children glue the ends of craft sticks together to make simple shapes such as squares or triangles. To hold the sticks in place until the glue dries, have the children clamp the ends together with spring-type clothespins. Point out how the clothespin clamps work like extra pairs of hands.

Simple Bird Feeder — Let older children enjoy making this simple bird feeder. Set out one 12-inch square of thin plywood, four 11-inch lengths of one-by-one, four screw eyes, glue and twine. Have the children glue and clamp the wood strips to the top edges of the plywood square. When the glue has dried, have them insert one screw eye in each corner of the square. Help the children string twine through each screw eye and tie it. Then hang the bird feeder outside and fill it with birdseed.

Carpentry Fun

Sawing

Sawing Practice — Before letting your children saw wood, have them practice sawing through large pieces of plastic foam or several thick pieces of cardboard. First, clamp the plastic foam or cardboard pieces to your workbench. Then let each child have a turn using a hand saw or a coping saw to saw through the materials.

Sawing Wood — Give your children many supervised opportunities to saw through wood. To help a child saw in a straight line, first draw a guideline on the wood with a pencil and a carpenter's square.

Measuring

Measuring Practice — Set out rulers, yardsticks and measuring tapes. Let your children use the tools to practice measuring the heights, widths or lengths of objects around the room, including chairs, tables and their own bodies. Ask questions such as these: "Which table is longer? Which is wider? Is your foot actually one foot long? How tall are you?"

Working With Squares — Cover a table completely with paper. Set out pencils and measuring tools called squares. Let your children practice drawing lines on the paper, using the squares as guides. Later, add wood pieces or boxes and let the children measure the sides and ends.

Carpentry Art

Carpentry Collage — Set out a 2-by-3-foot piece of plywood and a variety of wood scraps. Let your children nail or glue the scraps to the plywood to make a group carpentry collage.

Tin-Punch Designs — On canning jar lids (or lids from frozen juice cans), draw dotted outlines of simple shapes. Place the lids on wood blocks and show your children how to lightly hammer a nail through each dot to create see-through designs. Punch a hole in the top of each lid and tie on a loop of yarn for hanging.

Sawdust Clay — Combine 2 cups flour and 4 cups hot water. Mix until thick and clear. Stir in fine sawdust until the mixture resembles modeling clay. Let your children create sculptures with the clay. When the sculptures have dried and hardened, have the children sand and paint them, if desired.

Carpentry Fun

Carpentry Art

Wooden Paperweights — Give each child a cross section of a small tree trunk. Have the children nail or glue bits of wood or wood shavings to the tops of their tree-trunk sections to make paperweights. When the glue has dried, let the children paint their paperweights, if desired.

Wood Curl Collages — Provide your children with wood shavings. Or help them make pencil shavings with hand-held pencil sharpeners. Then have the children glue the shavings on plastic-foam food trays to make collages.

Note Holders — Let your children make these simple note holders. Have each child place a wooden paint-stirring stick horizontally on a table. Then have the child glue three spring-type clothes-pins, clip ends pointed down, to the stick—one in the middle and one at each end. When the glue has dried, let the children paint their note holders or decorate them with stickers, if desired.

Carpentry Learning Games

Weighing Nails — Set out a scale, a bucket of nails and a small scoop. Let your children experiment with weighing the nails. Ask them to find out how many nails there are in one pound.

Short and Long Nails — Set out 10 nails of various lengths. Let your children take turns arranging the nails from shortest to longest or longest to shortest.

Tool Match-Ups — Trace around your carpentry tools on a large piece of posterboard or on separate cardboard squares. Let your children match the tools to the shape outlines.

Sandpaper Match-Ups — Cut two squares each from the following grades of sandpaper: extra-fine, fine, medium and coarse. Mix up the squares and let your children try matching them by touch.

Carpentry Fun

Carpentry Learning Games

Wood Sort — In a box, place small objects made of wood and small items made of other materials. Let your children sort the objects into two groups.

Feelie Bag — In a bag, place familiar wooden items such as a clothespin, a block, a craft stick, a spoon, a pencil and a large bead. Let each child reach into the bag and try to identify the different objects by touch.

Carpentry Sort — Ask your children to bring in assorted hardware items such as nails, screws, hooks and hinges. Place the hardware in a large bucket in the carpentry center. When you have a good supply, let the children take turns sorting the items by kind into separate boxes.

Nuts and Bolts Sort — Set out three containers. Place nuts of various sizes in one container and matching bolts in another. Have your children take turns finding the matching nuts and bolts, screwing them together and placing the pairs in the third container.

I'm a Builder

Sung to: "Frere Jacques"

I'm a builder, I'm a builder,
Build, build, build,
Build, build, build.
Building homes is what I do,
Watch me while I build a few.
Build, build, build,
Build, build, build.

Here's my hammer, here's my hammer,
Pound, pound, pound,
Pound, pound, pound.
Pounding nails is what I do,
Watch me while I pound a few.
Pound, pound, pound,
Pound, pound, pound.

Here's my saw, here's my saw,
Saw, saw, saw,
Saw, saw, saw.
Sawing boards is what I do,
Watch me while I saw a few.
Saw, saw, saw,
Saw, saw, saw.

Elizabeth McKinnon

See What I Made Today

Sung to: "Oh Dear, What Can the
    Matter Be?"

I love to hammer wood,
I love to hammer wood,
I love to hammer wood.
See what I made today.

I love to sand wood,
I love to sand wood,
I love to sand wood.
See what I made today.

I love to glue wood,
I love to glue wood,
I love to glue wood.
See what I made today.

I love to saw wood,
I love to saw wood,
I love to saw wood.
See what I made today.

Jean Warren

Carpentry Fun

Learning With Trees

Arm Tree Prints

Making the Trees — Give each of your children a large piece of light-blue construction paper. Help one child at a time brush brown paint on his or her palm, fingers and inside forearm. Then show the child how to press his or her arm and hand on the paper to make a print of a tree with five "branches." Set the children's tree prints aside to dry.

Leafy Trees — Give the children their Arm Tree Prints. Set out containers of green paint or paint in autumn colors such as red, yellow and orange. Let your children dip small pieces of sponge into the paint and dab them on their tree prints to make leaves.

Blossoming Trees — Set out containers of pink and white paint. Let your children sponge-print clouds of spring blossoms onto their tree prints.

Paper Trees

Making the Trees — For each of your children, cut a bare tree shape out of brown construction paper. Have the children glue their tree shapes on pieces of light-blue or white construction paper.

Torn Paper Leaves — Give your children, scraps of green, red, yellow or orange construction paper. Let them tear the scraps into small pieces and glue them on their paper trees for leaves. Or have the children add leaves by gluing on torn pieces of colored tissue paper.

Popcorn Blossoms — In an area away from children, shake 2 cups popped popcorn in a bag with 1 tablespoon each of powdered red and white tempera paint. Let your children glue the pink popcorn puffs on their paper tree pictures to create spring blossoms.

Learning With Trees

Autumn Leaf Prints

Give each of your children several fresh autumn leaves. Let the children paint the front sides of their leaves with red, yellow and orange paint. Have them arrange their painted leaves on pieces of cardboard (painted side up), cover the leaves with pieces of black construction paper, and rub across the papers with their hands. Then have them carefully lift their black papers to reveal colorful autumn leaf prints.

Leaf Rubbings

Let your children help collect an assortment of leaves. Attach the leaves to a tabletop with loops of tape rolled sticky side out. Have the children take turns making rubbings by placing pieces of newsprint on top of the leaves and coloring over them with the sides of unwrapped crayons.

Sawdust Pictures

Let your children paint designs with glue on pieces of construction paper. While the glue is still wet, have the children place their papers in shallow box lids and sprinkle on sawdust. After waiting a bit, have them lift their papers and tap the excess sawdust back into the box lids. When the glue has dried, display the Sawdust Pictures on a wall or a bulletin board.

Variation: Instead of sawdust, use wood shavings that are sold for pet bedding.

Evergreen Branch Painting

Set out several different kinds of evergreen branches that have been cut into short lengths. Let your children take turns painting at an easel, using the branches instead of brushes. As the children work, talk about the colors, textures and scents of the different evergreens.

Variation: Let your children try painting with different kinds of pine cones.

Twig Frames

Make a picture frame for each child by cutting a 7-by-9½-inch rectangle out of the center of an 8½-by-11-inch piece of cardboard. Set out an assortment of small twigs. Let your children glue the twigs around the outside edges of their cardboard frames. Then help them tape pieces of artwork to the back sides of their frames, if desired.

Bark Rubbings

Give your children pieces of newsprint and unwrapped crayons, then take them on a nature walk. Whenever the children spot a tree that has unusual looking bark, let them make rubbings. Have them place their papers against the trunk of the tree and color over them with the sides of their crayons. When you return from your walk, encourage the children to compare and discuss their Bark Rubbings.

Pressed Leaves

Have your children collect autumn leaves in various colors. Cut waxed paper into identical squares. Let each child arrange several leaves, along with some colorful crayon shavings, between two of the squares. Then place the squares between two pieces of cloth and press them with a warm iron to seal the papers together. If desired, frame the children's papers before hanging them in a window.

Variation: Have your children arrange their leaves without the crayon shavings. When all the papers have been sealed, staple them together to make a pressed leaf book for your science corner.

Note: Activities that involve the use of electrical appliances require adult supervision at all times.

Four Seasons Placemats

Give each child four identical pictures of a bare tree drawn on pieces of light-blue construction paper. Talk with your children about the changes a tree goes through during the year. Then let them decorate their pictures with crayons or paint to show how a tree would look in fall, winter, spring and summer. Cover the pictures with clear self-stick paper. Let your children use their pictures as seasonal placemats at snack time.

Tree Facts

■ Trees are the largest of all plants.

■ The bark of a tree protects it, similar to how our skin protects our bodies.

■ The trunk of a tree supports the rest of the tree, just as our spine gives us our shape.

■ A tree needs water, air and nutrients, just as we do.

■ The roots of a tree grow underground and keep it from falling over, just as our legs and feet help us to keep our balance and stand straight and tall.

■ Deciduous trees grow fruits and nuts. Evergreen trees (conifers) grow seed cones.

Tree Safari

Before You Go — Before taking your children on a Tree Safari to a park or other nature area, explain that some trees grow leaves and are called deciduous trees while others grow needles and are called evergreen trees.

On the Way — Whenever your children spot an interesting tree on your safari, have them try answering the following questions: "Is the bark rough or smooth? Can you wrap your arms around the tree and tell how wide it is? What color is the tree? Does it have leaves or needles? Would you say the tree is short or tall?"

When You Return — After you get back from your safari, ask your children to tell what they learned about trees while you list their responses. Use the list to make a chart for the children to illustrate.

Seasonal Changes

With your children, locate a deciduous tree in your neighborhood and make a special point of visiting it every month or so. Help your children keep a record of the changes that they observe in the tree throughout the year. Let them work together to make seasonal charts that include their own illustrations as well as photographs of the tree.

Extension: Let your children help you collect leaves from your special tree along with leaves from other kinds of deciduous trees. Discuss how the leaves are alike and different.

Life Cycle of a Tree

On six large index cards, draw pictures that illustrate the life cycle of an apple tree. Include pictures of a seed in the ground, a tree seedling, a tree in bud, a tree in blossom, a tree with young apples growing on it, and a ripe apple cut in half with the seeds revealed. Use the cards to help your children understand how an apple tree makes its own seeds for starting new apple trees. Then mix up the cards and let the children take turns arranging them in the proper sequence.

Hug a Tree Today

Why not hug a tree today
Or pat it on its bark?
Give a tree a great big squeeze
At home or in the park.

Find the tree you like the best
And stand beneath its shade.
Stretch your arms around its trunk
And hug until you fade.

Imagine the birds
That have lived in your tree,
Imagine the squirrel in its nest.
A tree is a home to all that come,
The perfect place to rest.

So put your arms around your tree,
Whether it's short or tall.
Hug your tree—you'll feel so good,
Winter, spring, summer or fall.

Susan M. Paprocki

Tree Puppet

Give each child one half of a paper plate. Let the children use crayons or felt-tip markers to color their plate halves green. Next, give each child a toilet tissue tube with a hole cut in one side, about 1 inch from the bottom, and two slits cut directly opposite each other at the top. Let the children color their tubes brown. When they have finished, help them insert their paper plate halves into the slits in their tubes to complete their trees. Show them how to poke a finger through the hole in each tube to resemble an animal peeking out of a hollow tree. Let them use their Tree Puppets when making up stories or singing songs.

Hint: If desired, use grease pencils to draw animal faces on the children's fingers.

Forest Friends

Using the patterns on pages 86-93, cut the following shapes out of felt: an evergreen tree, a deer, a mouse, a bird, a skunk and a squirrel. Cut the following shapes from felt to place on the felt evergreen tree as decorations: bells, red berries, white and green flowers, and brown nuts. Also cut a piece of red string to add to the tree. Use the shapes on your flannelboard as you tell the story that follows.

In the woods, not far away,
Some children came one winter day
To decorate a tree so fair,
With gifts the animals could share.

They covered it with bells and berries
And other things to make it merry.
Flowers, nuts and bright red string
For the animals they did bring.

The tree felt very, very proud
And wanted so to shout out loud
And say, "How beautiful am I!"
When a mother deer walked by.

With gentle eyes she blinked and stared,
And then, so cautiously, she dared
To take the bells off of the tree.
She said, "I'll take these home with me.

"I'll put them on my baby deer
So I will know that he is near.
The bells will jingle if he strays,
And I will find him right away."

Then as she set out for her house,
There scampered up a little mouse.
He spied the berries red and sweet
And said, "I'll take these home to eat."

Just then the tiny mouse, he heard
The flutter of a winter bird,
Who perched up high so she could see
The string that hung upon the tree.

She took the string so soft and red
To line her nest and warm her bed.
But just before her wings were spread,
She saw a black-and-white-striped head.

A skunk approached with tail held high,
His nose was up, he wasn't shy.
He saw the flowers white and green
And said, "They smell so fresh and clean.

"I think I'll wear one by my ear,
Perhaps my friends will then come near.
I don't know why they run away
Whenever I come out to play."

The skunk ran quickly through the trees.
The wind picked up, and with the breeze
The snow began to dance and swirl.
And through the snowflakes came a squirrel.

She scurried round and searched the ground
For any food that could be found.
And when she came upon the tree,
Big brown nuts she then did see.

She took them slowly, one by one,
And walked away—she did not run.
She did not want to lose the treat
The children left for her to eat.

Soon all the treats were gone that day,
But the animals came back to play.
What a lovely time of year
When treats are shared and friends are near!

Adapted by Jean Warren
From a story by DeeDee Crocket

High in the Tree

Cut a large, bare tree shape out of brown felt, five leaf shapes out of red felt, four bird shapes out of blue felt, three tree frog shapes out of green felt, two squirrel shapes out of gray felt and one owl shape out of yellow felt. Place the tree on a flannelboard and put the other shapes on the tree. Then recite the following poem, letting your children fill in the blank after each verse.

Red leaves, red leaves,
High in the tree.
How many red leaves
Do you see? _____

Blue birds, blue birds,
High in the tree.
How many blue birds
Do you see? _____

Green frogs, green frogs,
High in the tree.
How many green frogs
Do you see? _____

Gray squirrels, gray squirrels,
High in the tree.
How many gray squirrels
Do you see? _____

Yellow owl, yellow owl,
High in the tree.
How many yellow owls
Do you see? _____

Jean Warren

Leaf Counting Game

Cut a bare tree shape out of brown felt and place it on a flannelboard. Cut 10 to 20 small leaf shapes out of green felt. Let your children take turns placing different numbers of leaves on the tree. Each time you remove the leaves, count them with the group.

Variation: Use a felt-tip marker to color a long white glove brown. Attach loops of tape rolled sticky side out to the backs of green felt leaf shapes. Slip on the glove to turn your hand and arm into a "tree" and let your children attach the leaves to the finger "branches."

Leaf Graphing

Prepare a simple graph by drawing a grid on a large piece of paper. Glue a different-colored leaf on each of the left-hand squares of the grid. Set out a variety of matching colored leaves and have the children sort them into separate piles. Count all the leaves of one color with the children. Then help them find the matching colored leaf on the graph and color in one square for each leaf of that color from the pile. Continue until all the leaves have been counted and recorded on the graph.

Variation: Make a graph for recording numbers of different-shaped leaves.

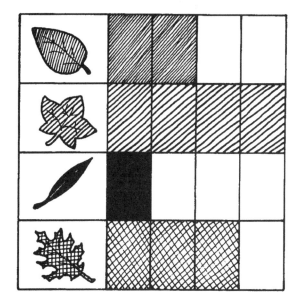

Counting Tree Rings

Bring in a cross section of a tree trunk. Point out the rings, explaining that each one represents a year in the life of the tree. Note that some rings are wider than others, indicating years when the tree grew a lot. Then help your children count the rings to discover how old the tree was.

Extension: Cut eight circles out of posterboard or cardboard and divide them into four pairs. On each pair of circles, draw matching numbers of rings to represent tree rings. Mix up the circles and let your children take turns finding the match-ups.

Let's Pretend

■ Ask your children to sit on the floor. First, have them pretend to be tiny acorns in the ground by rolling themselves into little balls. Have them slowly extend their roots, or legs, and then gradually push their heads up through pretend soil into sunlight, with their arms held at their sides. As they grow taller and taller, have them extend their arm "branches" out at their sides. Finally, have them stretch their arms up over their heads as they become full-grown oak trees.

■ While the trees are standing together in a leafy grove, talk them through different kinds of weather conditions. Ask: "How do you move when a light breeze blows through your branches? When the wind blows and the rain falls? How do you look when snow covers your branches? When it's a hot day with no breeze at all?"

■ While your children are still pretending to be trees, have them use their imaginations to answer questions such as these: "How do you feel when birds fly around your heads? When they build nests in your branches? How do you feel when squirrels scamper up and down your trunks? When they pick your acorns? How do you feel when children come to sit under your branches and read or play games?"

Woodcutting Game

Divide your children into two groups and let them take turns being Trees and Woodcutters. Let the Woodcutters pretend to saw back and forth on the Trees as everyone counts to 20. When the Woodcutters call "Timber!" have the Trees topple over. Then have the Trees and the Woodcutters trade places and start the game again.

Learning With Trees

Trees

Elm trees stretch and stretch so wide.

(Hold arms out at sides.)

Their limbs reach out on every side.

Pine trees stretch and stretch so high.

(Hold arms straight up.)

They nearly reach up to the sky.

Willows droop and droop so low.

(Bend over and lower arms.)

Their branches sweep the ground below.

Author Unknown

Oak Tree

As you read the poem below, encourage your children to act out the lines any way they wish.

Here is an oak tree straight and tall,

And here are its branches wide.

Here is a nest of twigs and moss,

With three little birds inside.

The breezes blow and the little leaves play,

But the branches hold the nest —

As they sway and bob and rock,

So the little birds can rest.

Author Unknown

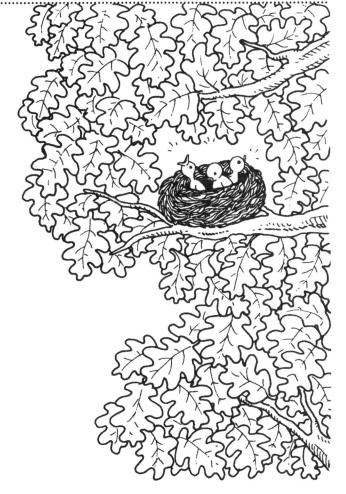

Learning With Trees

Trees Are Growing

Sung to: "The Farmer in the Dell"

The trees are growing high,

> (Raise arms overhead, fingers touching.)

The trees are growing high.

With soil and rain and sunny days,

The trees are growing high.

The trees are growing roots,

> (Bend over and touch floor.)

The trees are growing roots.

With soil and rain and sunny days,

The trees are growing roots.

The trees are growing bark,

> (Run hands up and down sides.)

The trees are growing bark.

With soil and rain and sunny days,

The trees are growing bark.

Additional Verses: The trees are growing branches, (Extend arms at sides); The trees are growing leaves, (Flutter fingers).

Susan Peters

Do You Know Who Lives in My Tree?

Sung to: "The Muffin Man"

Do you know who lives in my tree,

Lives in my tree, lives in my tree?

Do you know who lives in my tree?

It is a little squirrel.

Continue with similar verses, substituting animal names such as bird, ant or owl, for squirrel.

Jean Warren

Have You Seen a Tree?

Sung to: "Did You Ever See a Lassie?"

Have you seen a tree in autumn,

In autumn, in autumn,

Have you seen a tree in autumn

With leaves falling down?

There are yellow leaves and red leaves

And orange leaves and brown leaves.

Have you seen a tree in autumn

With leaves falling down?

Have you seen a tree in winter,

In winter, in winter,

Have you seen a tree in winter

With branches bare and brown?

Where leaves are expected

The snow has collected.

Have you seen a tree in winter

With branches bare and brown?

Have you seen a tree in springtime,

In springtime, in springtime,

Have you seen a tree in springtime

With new budding leaves?

Bird babies are resting,

On new branches nesting.

Have you seen a tree in springtime

With new budding leaves?

Have you seen a tree in summer,

In summer, in summer,

Have you seen a tree in summer

All covered with fruit?

There just is no stopping

Some ripe fruit from dropping.

Have you seen a tree in summer

All covered with fruit?

Diane Thom

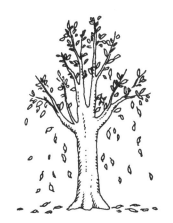 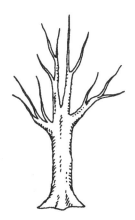  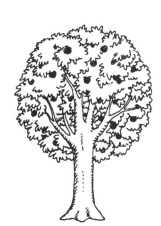

What Is a Tree?

A Tree Is a Home — Discuss with your children how a tree can be a home to different animals such as birds, squirrels and insects. Be sure to emphasize the trees and animals in your area.

A Tree Is a Provider — With your children, make a list of all the things we get from trees. Your list might include things such as these: wood for building fires to keep us warm; wood for making houses, furniture, toys, etc.; flowers, fruits and nuts; paper and paper products; shade for keeping us cool on hot days; and protection from wind, snow and rain.

A Tree Creates Jobs — Talk about people whose jobs depend upon trees such as woodcutters, carpenters, furniture makers and wood carvers. Let your children act out these jobs and explain what they are doing or making.

Learning With Trees

40

Tree Treats

Each day for one week, let your children help you prepare a snack using a different fruit that grows on trees. For example, your week's menu might include baked apples, banana bread, peach yogurt, grapefruit juice and frozen orange pops. Other fruits you could use include pears, plums, apricots and dates.

Extension: Let your children sample other foods from trees such as olives, nuts and chocolate (which is made from the seeds of the cacao tree).

Tree Cookies

Use a favorite recipe to make sugar cookies. Roll out the dough and let your children cut out tree shapes with Christmas tree cookie cutters. Bake the cookies according to your recipe directions. Then let the children decorate their tree cookies with green frosting.

In the Forest

Forest Facts

■ Forests cover about one-third of our earth.

■ There are different kinds of forests such as hardwood forests, softwood forests, swamp forests and tropical rain forests.

■ Forests help provide us with water by acting like sponges and holding the rainfall in the ground. In high areas, they shade the snow so that it melts slowly, thus keeping streams of water flowing year-round.

■ Forests act like giant air conditioners. They cool surrounding areas with their shade and the moisture that is given off by their leaves and needles.

■ Forests clean and enrich the air we breathe. Their leaves and needles take in carbon dioxide and give out oxygen.

■ Forests provide food and shelter for thousands of animals and insects.

Measuring the Difference

Talk with your children about how forests act like huge air conditioners (see Forest Facts on this page). On a hot day, take your children outside. Help them use an outdoor thermometer to measure the temperature in direct sunlight. Then carry the thermometer to a shady spot under some trees. Wait a few minutes, then measure the temperature again. Discuss how much the trees help to lower the temperature and make the air feel cooler.

In the Forest

Forest Community

Display pictures of a North American forest. Talk with your children about how the forest is a community of trees and other living things. Explain that on the forest floor is a carpet of decaying leaves, moss and small twigs. On top of that is a layer of logs, fallen branches and plants. Insects live in and feed on the rotting logs and leaves, while small animals live in the larger hollowed-out logs and tree stumps. Larger animals roam the forest, living off the plants and smaller animals. At the top of the forest, leaves and needles make food for the trees while providing places for birds to rest and build their nests.

Forest Terrarium

To help your children visualize a forest, try this. Set out a large glass terrarium. Place several inches of rich soil in the bottom of the tank and let the children help plant a few tree seedlings and small ferns. After sprinkling on water, have the children add crumbled leaves, evergreen needles, twigs or small branches, and pieces of moss. Place small ceramic or plastic forest animals inside the tank to complete your Forest Terrarium.

Variation: Instead of real plants, use small artificial evergreen trees and ferns, available at hobby or craft stores.

In the Forest

Forest Mural

Cut several large sponges into triangles and set out a piece of butcher paper. Let your children dip the sponge shapes into green tempera paint and press them all over the butcher paper to make a forest of evergreen trees. When the paint has dried, hang the paper on a wall at the children's eye level. Make copies of the forest animal patterns on pages 86-93. Have the children color the animal pictures as desired. Then cut out the pictures and let the children tape them to the butcher paper.

Forest Flannelboard Game

Cut evergreen tree shapes out of felt and arrange them on a flannelboard to create a forest scene. Cut out pictures of forest animals from nature magazines. Glue the pictures on heavy paper, trim around the edges, and attach felt strips to the backs. Have your children sit with you around the flannelboard and give them each a picture to hold. Then start telling a story about the forest and the animals that live there. Each time you introduce an animal into your story, have the child holding that animal picture place it on the flannelboard. Continue until all the animals have been placed in the forest scene.

Variation: Put the animal pictures into a bag and start telling a story about the forest. As each child in turn takes a picture from the bag and places it on the flannelboard, introduce that animal into your story.

In the Forest

Forest Tree Facts

■ Trees are the biggest plants on Earth. The largest is the giant sequoia (from one sequoia, up to 40 houses could be built). The tallest tree is the California redwood, which can grow as high as 400 feet.

■ Trees can live longer than any human being or animal.

■ The roots of trees hold the soil to the earth and help prevent erosion and flooding.

■ Groups of trees can shield out strong winds and loud noises.

■ Forests are a renewable resource. As trees are cut down, new seedlings can be planted to take their place.

Plant a Forest

Paint a shoe box brown and cut six slits in the lid. Number the slits from 1 to 6. Cut six evergreen tree shapes from green construction paper. Number the trees by drawing one pine cone on one shape, two pine cones on another shape, three pine cones on a third shape, and so on. Attach the tree shapes to craft sticks. Let your children count the numbers of pine cones on the trees. Then have them insert the trees into the matching numbered slits in the shoe box lid.

Small Forest Plants

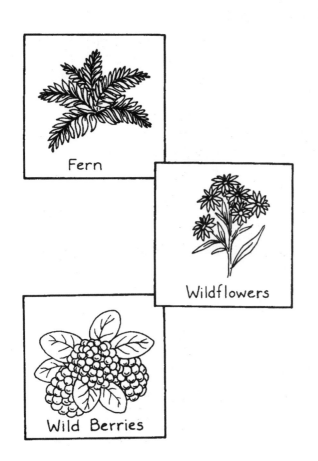

Fern

Wildflowers

Wild Berries

Explain to your children that there are many plants other than trees in the forest. Some of the most common are ferns, wildflowers and wild berries. Collect pictures of these plants and display them around the room. Then make paper cutouts of the plants and let your children add them to their Forest Mural (see page 46).

Fern Rubbings

Arrange real or artificial fern fronds flat on a table. Set out pieces of newsprint and unwrapped green crayons. Let your children place the papers on top of the fern fronds and color over them with the sides of the crayons to make rubbings.

Wildflower Mural

Make paint pads by placing folded paper towels in shallow containers and pouring on small amounts of different-colored tempera paint. Set out rubber stamps in the shapes of various flowers. Place a piece of butcher paper on a low table or on the floor. Let your children use the stamps with the paint pads to make flower prints all over the butcher paper. When the paint has dried, have the children use green crayons or felt-tip markers to add stems, leaves and moss. Display the finished mural on a wall or a bulletin board.

Forest Snacks

Let your children sample foods that come from the forest. For example, set out pine nuts and canned mushrooms along with blackberries or other forest berries for them to taste. If actual berries are not available, use berry jams or jellies.

In the Forest

What's on the Forest Floor?

Explain to your children that on the forest floor are mushrooms, tree stumps, hollow logs, and blankets of fallen leaves and moss. Nestled around, inside and beneath all of this are creatures such as toads, slugs, centipedes, spiders, worms, grubs, beetles and ants. The larger of these creatures use the stumps and hollow logs for homes, while the smaller ones live beneath rotting bark. Worms, grubs and centipedes are busy all day chewing up fallen leaves to make new soil for the plants that grow on the forest floor.

Making New Soil

Set out a pan of dirt along with dried leaves, small twigs, tree bark and dried evergreen needles. Let your children pretend that they are worms or grubs busy making new soil. Have them crumble or grind the leaves, twigs, bark and needles into tiny pieces. Then have them mix the pieces with the dirt in the pan. Later, add the new soil to an outside garden.

Hollow Log Home

Use a long cardboard carton to make a pretend hollow log. Cut several large, round holes in the sides of the carton. Then let your children help paint the carton dark brown. Glue pieces of green felt on the outside and inside of the carton for moss. When the glue has dried, have the children pretend to be small forest animals living and playing in their Hollow Log Home.

Forest Art

Mossy Branches — Bring in pieces of moss for your children to touch and examine. Explain that in the forest, moss grows on the ground, rocks, logs, and even the sides of trees. Then give your children small branches of wood and let them glue on green sponge pieces for moss.

Mushroom Prints — Place folded paper towels in shallow containers. Mix brown and white tempera paint together and pour small amounts over the paper towels to make paint pads. Cut large mushrooms in half lengthwise. Let your children press the mushroom halves on the paint pads and use them to make prints on pieces of light-green construction paper.

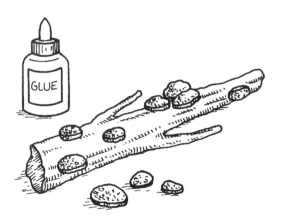

In the Forest

Tree Friends
Sung to: "Down in the Valley"

Deep in the forest
With trees so tall,
I feel so little,
So very small.

I love to look up
And see the trees bend,
I know they are saying,
"Let us be friends."

Jean Warren

Down in the Forest
Sung to: "Down by the Station"

Down in the forest
Early in the morning,
See the little plants
Bending to and fro.
See the gentle breeze
Help them raise their arms.
Swish-swish, swish-swish,
Wave hello!

Down in the forest
Early in the morning,
See the little animals
Scurry to and fro.
See the little frog
Jump up on a mushroom.
Ribbet, ribbet,
Off he goes!

Jean Warren

Sensing the Forest

Sung to: "My Bonnie Lies Over the Ocean"

I love the sounds of the forest,

The water, the birds and the leaves.

I also love the silence

That fills my world of trees.

Trees, trees, trees, trees,

That fills my world of trees, trees, trees.

Trees, trees, trees, trees,

That fills my world of trees.

I love the smells of the forest,

The pine and the flowers so sweet.

I love the smells of the forest,

They smell so fresh to me.

Me, me, me, me,

They smell so fresh to me, to me.

Me, me, me, me,

They smell so fresh to me.

I love the feel of the forest,

The moss, the ferns and the trees.

I love the feel of the forest,

It feels just right to me.

Me, me, me, me,

It feels just right to me, to me.

Me, me, me, me,

It feels just right to me.

I love the sights of the forest,

The streams, the flowers and leaves.

I love to watch the sunlight,

Dancing from tree to tree.

Tree, tree, tree, tree,

Dancing from tree to tree, tree, tree.

Tree, tree, tree, tree,

Dancing from tree to tree.

I love the tastes of the forest,

The berries, the honey from bees.

I love the tastes of the forest,

At breakfast, dinner or tea.

Tea, tea, tea, tea,

At breakfast, dinner or tea, tea, tea.

Tea, tea, tea, tea,

At breakfast, dinner or tea.

Jean Warren

In the Forest

Forest Animals

Bear Facts

■ Bears are mammals. They have thick fur and bulky bodies. Their legs are short and powerful.

■ Bears usually move at a lumbering walk, but they can run as fast as 30 miles an hour. They can also climb trees and swim.

■ Bears live from 15 to 30 years in the wild.

■ Favorite foods of bears include fish, ants, berries, fruits, nuts and honey.

■ Most bears spend the winter sleeping in caves, hollow logs or other kinds of dens.

■ The American black bear weighs up to 500 pounds and appears in a variety of colors, in spite of its name.

■ The grizzly bear weighs up to 1,000 pounds. Its coat color ranges from yellowish to almost black. Today, only a small number of grizzlies can be found in the northwest forests of North America.

Fuzzy Bears

Cut a bear shape for each child out of brown construction paper or posterboard. (See pattern on page 88.) Let your children brush glue all over their shapes. Then have them sprinkle sawdust on top of the glue to represent fur.

Variation: Instead of sawdust, let the children sprinkle on used tea leaves or coffee grounds that have been rinsed and dried.

Fishing Game

Cut fish shapes for each of your children out of red, yellow and blue construction paper (or use any colors desired). Make a "river" by arranging two long pieces of blue yarn on the floor about a foot apart. Place the fish in the river and have the children pretend to be bears. Ask each one in turn to catch a red fish, a yellow fish, etc. Let the "bears" keep the fish that they catch, making sure that everyone ends up with the same number of shapes.

Variation: Write different numerals on the fish shapes to make a number recognition game.

The Bears Are Walking

Sung to: "When Johnny Comes Marching Home"

The bears are walking through the woods

Today, today.

The bears are walking through the woods

To eat and play.

They catch some fish and eat them too.

They munch on berries, quite a few.

Then they run around and climb a tree or two.

Jean Warren

Forest Animals

Bird Facts

■ Birds are warm-blooded vertebrates (animals with backbones). They lay eggs from which their young hatch. Birds have no teeth. They use their hard beaks or bills to get and eat food.

■ Birds are the only animals that are covered with feathers.

■ Because most birds can fly, they are found all over the world in forests, mountains, deserts and ocean areas.

■ Using their wings, birds can travel faster than all other animals. The fastest bird can fly up to 100 miles an hour. Not all birds can fly; some walk, run or swim.

■ Many birds migrate, or travel long distances, to warmer areas during the winter months.

Feathered Birds

Cut a bird shape for each of your children out of the desired color of construction paper. (See patterns on page 92.) Set out feathers and small containers of tempera paint. Let the children dip the feathers into the paint and brush it all over their bird shapes. When they have finished, let them each tape several feathers to their painted birds.

Bird Nests

In springtime, give each of your children a brown paper lunch bag and take them on a walk. Along the way, have the children put into their bags items that birds might use to build nests, such as twigs, leaves and pieces of string. When you return from the walk, help the children fold down the sides of their bags to form "nests." Then have them place their bags outside so that birds can use the contents for nest building.

See the Birds

Sung to: "Frere Jacques"

See the birds, see the birds,

In the trees, in the trees.

They have stopped to rest,

Some are building nests,

In the trees, in the trees.

Repeat, each time substituting a specific bird type, such as *robins*, *crows* or *pigeons*, for *birds*.

Jean Warren

Deer Facts

■ Deer are mammals. Some deer live deep in the forest, while others live close to highways and populated areas.

■ In North America, the white-tailed deer is the most common member of the deer family. When alarmed, it raises its tail, showing the white hairs that grow on the tail's underside.

■ Adult male deer are called bucks. White-tailed bucks stand about 3½ feet high at the shoulder and weigh 120 to 150 pounds.

■ Adult female deer, or does, are smaller and lighter in weight than bucks. Their babies are called fawns.

■ Most male deer grow antlers that have many branches and end in points.

■ The foods deer eat include leaves, grass, bark, nuts, vegetables and fruits.

Flashlight Freeze

Let your children pretend to be deer and have them prance in place. Shine a flashlight on and off. Whenever the "deer" see the light, have them raise their heads high and freeze. When the light goes out, have them start prancing again. Continue the game as long as interest lasts.

Antler Matching

Cut a deer shape with antlers out of several different colors of construction paper. (See pattern on page 89.) Cover the shapes with clear self-stick paper for durability, if desired. Cut the antlers off the deer shapes and place them in a separate pile. Let your children take turns lining up the deer shapes and placing the matching-colored antlers above each deer head.

Little Deer

Sung to: "Down by the Station"

Down in the woods

Early in the morning,

See the little deer

Looking for some food.

First they eat some leaves,

Then they eat some berries.

Munch, munch, crunch, crunch,

Off they go!

Jean Warren

Forest Animals

61

Owl Facts

■ Owls are found on almost every continent of the world.

■ There are more than 130 different kinds of owls.

■ Owls see very well in the dark. Their eyes are large and very sensitive to the dimmest light.

■ Owls cannot move their eyes from side to side, so they must move their heads to look at objects around them.

■ Most owls hunt by night and are meat eaters.

■ The "ears" on the tops of some owls' heads are actually little tufts of feathers.

■ Owls are farmers' friends because they eat mice and harmful insects that destroy crops.

Owl Puppets

Give each child a paper plate. Have your children color the backs of their plates with brown crayons or felt-tip markers to make owl heads. Give them yellow paper triangles to glue on their plates for beaks and yellow or white paper baking cups to glue on for eyes. If desired, let them color black circles in the centers of the baking cups to add expression. On the back side of each child's plate, staple half of another paper plate around the top rim to make an "envelope." To manipulate the puppet, have the child slip a hand inside the envelope and move his or her wrist back and forth. Encourage the children to use their Owl Puppets when telling stories or singing songs.

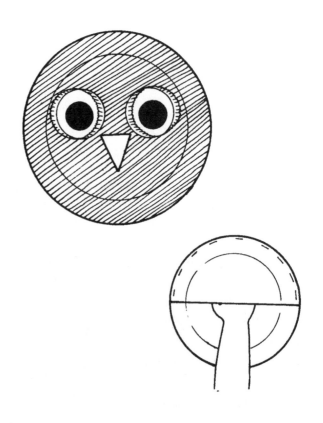

Owl Tag

Choose one child to be the Owl. While the other children close their eyes, let the Owl find a hiding place in the room. When the other children open their eyes, have the Owl make hooting sounds. Have the other children listen carefully and try to guess where the Owl is hiding. Let the first child to guess correctly be the Owl for the next round of the game.

Little Owl

Sung to: "This Old Man"

Little owl, in the tree,
He is winking down at me.
With a wink, wink, wink, wink,
All through the night,
Little owl is quite a sight!

Little owl, in the tree,
He is hooting down at me.
With a hoot, hoot, hoot, hoot,
All through the night,
Little owl is quite a sight!

Jean Warren

Forest Animals

Porcupine Facts

■ Porcupines are mammals. They are found in wooded areas throughout the world.

■ The bodies of porcupines are covered with long, needle-like quills that protect the animals from most predators.

■ Porcupines do not shoot their quills, as is commonly believed. Instead, they move their tails back and forth, which shakes the quills loose and sends them flying through the air.

■ Foods that porcupines eat include tree bark, leaves, evergreen needles and fruits.

■ Porcupines are nocturnal, which means they sleep during the day and are active at night.

Pine Cone Porcupines

Take your children on a walk to collect pine cones and dried pine needles. When you return, let the children press playdough all over the pine cones. Then have them stick short pieces of the pine needles into the playdough to create Pine Cone Porcupines.

Forest Animals

Prickly or Smooth?

Collect items that are prickly (a pine cone, an evergreen sprig, a hairbrush, a whisk broom, etc.) and items that are smooth (a posterboard square, a plastic plate, a marble, a piece of satin, etc.). Invite one child at a time to sit with you. While the child's eyes are closed, give him or her one item from each category to touch. Ask the child to tell you which item is prickly and which item is smooth. Continue in the same manner until all the items have been used.

Once There Was a Porcupine

Sung to: "Yankee Doodle"

Once there was a porcupine
Who lived beneath a tree.
Everyone would run from her,
What could the matter be?
She was lonely all the time,
No one stayed to play.
Why did everyone she meet
Have to run away?

Jean Warren

Forest Animals

Raccoon Facts

■ Raccoons are mammals. They use their front paws like little hands to search and dig for food. They also appear to enjoy touching and playing with small objects.

■ Raccoons eat a variety of foods such as fish, insects, fruits and nuts.

■ Raccoons are found mainly in forests in North and South America.

■ Raccoons are brownish-gray in color. They have long, bushy tails that are ringed with stripes. Their faces are pointed, and they look as though they are wearing masks because of the dark-colored fur around their eyes.

■ Raccoons make their homes both in trees and in nests on the ground.

Feelie Box

In a box, place five or six familiar objects such as a toy car, a crayon, a plastic egg, a soft sponge, an old toothbrush and a baby shoe. Have your children pretend to be raccoons. Let them each have a turn reaching into the box, grasping an object in their hands, and trying to identify it by touch. When the game is over, let the children find other objects around the room to place in the box. Then start the game again.

Seeing Stripes

Have your children look around the room or outside to find stripes in everyday objects. Encourage them to be creative. For example, besides stripes on clothing or a flag, they might see stripes formed by chair slats, window blinds, ladder rungs, ridges in corrugated cardboard, or lines on writing paper. Record the children's findings on a wall chart and have them count the kinds of stripes they have found.

Raccoon, Raccoon

Sung to: "Twinkle, Twinkle, Little Star"

Raccoon, raccoon, climbing a tree,

Wearing a mask, you can't fool me.

Hiding there so I can't see

What you're doing in that tree.

Raccoon, raccoon, climbing a tree,

Wearing a mask, you can't fool me.

Bonnie Woodard

Skunk Facts

■ Skunks are mammals. They are found only in North and South America.

■ Skunks have musk glands that store a foul-smelling liquid. When a skunk is threatened by another animal, it will spray the animal with this liquid. The liquid causes temporary blindness, allowing the skunk to escape.

■ Skunks help farmers by eating harmful insects. They also eat rodents, fruits, bulbs and eggs.

■ Most skunks live in underground dens, although some kinds of skunks can climb and live in trees.

■ Skunks are active at night and sleep during the day. During the cold winter months, they stay in their sleeping dens most of the time.

■ The most common species in North America is the striped skunk. About the size of a house cat, this skunk has shiny black fur with two white stripes down its back and one down its nose.

Black and White Fun

Let your children do one or more of the activities that follow.

- ■ Paint black-and-white pictures.
- ■ Draw on black construction paper with white chalk.
- ■ Draw on sheets of newspaper with black crayons.
- ■ Make black fingerprints on white paper.
- ■ Brush black paint over white crayon-resist drawings.

Sniffing Game

In separate yogurt cups or other non-transparent containers, place materials with familiar scents, such as peanut butter, chocolate, jelly, ketchup, mustard, a lemon wedge, a cinnamon stick, a small bar of soap, and a piece of peppermint gum. Let your children take turns closing their eyes and using their sense of smell to identify the contents of the containers.

Don't Scare a Skunk

Sung to: "Skip to My Lou"

Don't scare a skunk or sorry you'll be,

Don't scare a skunk or sorry you'll be,

Don't scare a skunk or sorry you'll be,

Sorry you'll be, my darling!

Betty Silkunas

Forest Animals

Squirrel Facts

■ Squirrels are mammals. There are more than 300 different kinds of squirrels.

■ Squirrels eat foods such as seeds, nuts, berries and fruits. Squirrels are known to gather bushels of pine cones during the fall and store them for the winter. They shred the cones to make bedding and eat the pine nuts that are found in the pine cones.

■ The most common North American squirrel is the tree squirrel, which has a thick, plumed tail. The tail acts like a balance when the squirrel leaps from branch to branch. Tree squirrels are gray, brown, tan or black in color. They live in holes in trees or build nests high in the branches.

■ Squirrels are found almost everywhere in the world except Madagascar, Australia and southern South America.

Pine Cone Hunt

Collect pine cones and hide them around the room where they can be found easily. Let your children pretend to be squirrels. Have them search for the cones while singing the song below. Each time they find a pine cone, have them put it into a box that you have set out to represent a storage place. When all the pine cones have been found, count them together with the children.

Sung to: "Ten Little Indians"

Little gray squirrels
Looking for pine cones,
Little gray squirrels
Looking for pine cones,
Little gray squirrels
Looking for pine cones,
Storing them away for winter.

Jean Warren

Forest Animals

Nut Sorting

Set out unshelled nuts such as pecans, walnuts, almonds, hazelnuts and Brazil nuts. Let your children sort the nuts by kind into separate containers. When they have finished, encourage them to count how many nuts there are of each kind.

Extension: Follow up by cracking the nuts and letting your children enjoy a nut snack.

I Saw a Little Squirrel

Sung to: "Did You Ever See a Lassie?"

I saw a little squirrel

A-pickin' up acorns.

I saw a little squirrel,

She ran up a tree.

She ran up and ran down

And ran up and ran down.

A busy little squirrel,

As busy as could be.

Becky Valenick

Wolf Facts

■ Wolves are mammals and members of the dog family. They have thick coats of fur and long, bushy tails. Their senses of smell and hearing are very good.

■ Wolves are meat eaters. They usually hunt in packs.

■ Wolves are thought to mate for life.

■ Gray wolves, or timber wolves, range in color from white to gray to black. Although they were once plentiful in the Northern Hemisphere, their numbers have been greatly reduced. Today in the United States, gray wolves are found mainly in Alaska.

■ Red wolves are smaller than gray wolves. They live in several places in the southern part of the United States.

■ Wolves live in burrows, which they usually dig into the dirt or snow. They also can be found living in small rock caves.

Wolf Paw Prints

Make several wolf paw-print stamps. For each stamp, cut a foot pad shape and four toe shapes out of thick cardboard. Glue the shapes in the correct positions (see illustration) to a block of wood. Make paint pads by placing folded paper towels in shallow containers and pouring on small amounts of tempera paint. Let your children dip the stamps into the paint and press them on pieces of construction paper to make Wolf Paw Prints.

Forest Animals

Wolf Family

Let your children play-act being a wolf family. Have the father and mother wolf share the work of digging their burrow. While the mother takes care of her newborn pups, have the father wolf bring her food and stand guard by their home. Encourage the pups to wrestle and play together. Then have the wolf parents take their pups out and show them how to find food for themselves.

Extension: While your children are still pretending to be wolves, let them make up stories about their adventures. Write down the stories on separate pieces of paper for the children to illustrate.

Little Wolf

Sung to: "Mary Had a Little Lamb"

Little wolf lives in a cave,

In a cave, in a cave.

Little wolf lives in a cave,

In the great big woods.

Little wolf likes to run and play,

Run and play, run and play.

Little wolf likes to run and play,

In the great big woods.

Little wolf eats mice and rabbits,

Mice and rabbits, mice and rabbits.

Little wolf eats mice and rabbits,

In the great big woods.

Jean Warren

Forest Preservation

Forest Fire Facts

■ There are 100,000 forest fires every year.

■ Most forest fires are caused by people.

■ Lightning bolts can start forest fires if they strike dry trees or grass.

■ Forest fires do more damage in windy weather because the wind blows the flames to other trees.

■ Many national forests have lookout stations that are built high above the trees. It is someone's job to live in a station, watch for fires, and alert firefighters.

■ Sometimes forest fires are hard to put out. They can burn for many days, leaving scorched, smoking land and homeless animals.

Fire Prevention Posters

Give each of your children a large piece of construction paper and a sprig of evergreen. Set out red, yellow and orange tempera paint. Let the children dip their evergreen sprigs into the paint and brush them across their papers to make flame pictures. When the paint has dried, help the children tape their evergreen sprigs to their papers. Use a black felt-tip marker to write "Prevent Forest Fires" on each child's paper. Then use the posters to make a fire prevention bulletin board display.

Forest Preservation

Introducing Smokey Bear

Contact your State Forester or regional office of the U.S. Department of Agriculture Forest Service to obtain Smokey Bear posters and other teaching aids. Use these materials to introduce your children to Smokey and his familiar message: "Only You Can Prevent Forest Fires." Talk about how Smokey teaches us that by preventing forest fires, we are conserving trees, protecting animal homes, and preserving the forests for everyone to enjoy.

I Do What Smokey Says

Sung to: "The Farmer in the Dell"

I do what Smokey says,

I do what Smokey says.

I care about our forests,

I do what Smokey says.

I do what Smokey says,

I do what Smokey says.

I don't play with matches,

I do what Smokey says.

I do what Smokey says,

I do what Smokey says.

I don't play with lighters,

I do what Smokey says.

Kathleen Cubley

Forest Preservation

Understanding Litter

On a tray, place several litter items (a plastic bag, an empty pop can, a wadded up piece of paper, a gum wrapper, etc.) and several nature items (a leaf, a rock, a pine cone, a twig, etc.). Explain to your children that litter is garbage that has not been put into a trash can. Talk about the items on the tray and help the children divide them into two groups: litter items and non-litter items. Then have them throw the litter items into a trash can and place the nature items outside on the ground.

Extension: Talk about how litter left in a forest can be harmful to the animals who live there. For example, some animals could get caught in plastic six-pack rings or cut by rusted cans, and some could become sick from eating garbage.

Woodsy Owl

Use materials from your State Forester to introduce your children to Woodsy Owl and his slogan: "Give a Hoot, Don't Pollute." Like Smokey Bear, Woodsy is a symbol of the U.S. Forest Service. He serves as a friendly reminder to take care of our air, water and land. After discussing Woodsy Owl, sing the song below with the children.

Sung to: "Yankee Doodle"

This great earth is our home,

It's up to us to care.

Woodsy Owl will lead the way,

Come on, let's do our share.

"Give a Hoot, Don't Pollute."

Clean land is best, we know.

Let's leave a trail that's nice and clean

Wherever we may go.

Kathleen Cubley

Picnic Time

Take your children to a park or a comfortable green area for a picnic. After eating, have the children gather all their garbage and throw it into a trash bag or garbage can. (Be sure to save the recyclables!) While the children are working, let them sing the song that follows.

Sung to: "Frere Jacques"

We're not litterbugs,

We're not litterbugs,

No siree, no siree!

We pick up our trash,

We pick up our trash,

Yes siree, yes siree!

Elizabeth McKinnon

Pick Up Your Litter

Sung to: "When Johnny Comes Marching Home"

Remember when you're in the woods,

Pick up your litter.

Remember that the woods are home

To lots of critters.

The deer, the beaver, the owl and bear,

All are thankful that you care.

So keep your litter

Out of their forest home.

Jean Warren

Forest Preservation

Understanding Air Pollution

Talk with your children about the importance of controlling air pollution. Explain that because tree leaves help purify the air by catching tiny particles of dust and other pollutants, we must make sure that we take good care of our trees and forests. To help the children understand what air pollution is, try this activity. Have them spread petroleum jelly on index cards. Then hang the cards in different locations outdoors and in your room. After at least one week, collect the cards. Examine and compare with the children the amounts of particles found on the different cards.

Save a Tree

Explain to your children that recycling a 3-foot stack of newspaper will save one tree from being cut down and turned into paper or paper products. Then place a piece of masking tape on a wall 3 feet above the floor. Have the children bring in newspapers and place them in a pile under the tape. Each time a 3-foot stack is collected for recycling, cut a tree shape out of one of the newspapers and let the children decorate it with green felt-tip markers. Display the trees around the room. Soon your children will be surrounded by a "forest" representing all the trees they have saved.

Tree of Life

Talk with your children about how trees in a forest provide food for the animals that live there. For example, birds eat fruit and seeds, deer graze on leaves and twigs, porcupines eat tree bark, squirrels eat nuts, and insects chew on roots and leaves. Then display a large picture of a tree. Have the children pretend to be different forest animals and take turns telling which part of the tree they would use for food.

Extension: Ask the "animals" to tell how they might use the tree for shelter.

Trees for Lunch

Sung to: "This Old Man"

Trees to munch, trees to crunch,

See the animals come for lunch.

With a munch, munch, crunch, crunch,

Watch them go!

Some eat fast and some eat slow.

Leaves to munch, leaves to crunch,

See the animals come for lunch.

With a munch, munch, crunch, crunch,

Watch them go!

Some eat fast and some eat slow.

Additional Verses: Berries to munch; Nuts to munch; Fruit to munch; Twigs to munch; Bark to munch; Roots to munch.

Jean Warren

Forest Preservation

Web of Life

Photocopy the forest patterns on pages 86-93. Cut out the patterns and give each of your children one to tape to his or her shirt. Have the children pretend to be the plants and animals shown on their shirts. Ask the children to stand in a circle. Give a large ball of yarn to one child. Have that child hold the yarn and toss the ball to another child. Repeat until each child is holding a section of the yarn and the web is complete. Explain to the children that the web represents the web of life in the forest. Each plant or animal is connected to all the others in some way. Then one at a time, have the children pretend that their plants or animals have disappeared from the forest and let go of the yarn. What happens to the web after one child lets go? After three children let go? After five? The web starts falling apart. When each part of the forest is taken care of, the web of life can stay together just as the yarn web did when all of the children were holding it.

Planting Tree Seedlings

Talk with your children about the importance of using our natural resources wisely and replacing what we use. Then let them plant tree seedlings in paper cups that have been filled with soil. When the seedlings are tall enough, transplant them outdoors and have the children water and care for them regularly.

Note: Packages of tree seedlings can be ordered from the National Arbor Day Foundation at a nominal cost. For information, write to: National Arbor Day Foundation, 211 N. 12th Street, Lincoln, NE 68508.

Reuse It!

Talk with your children about reusing products that come from trees. Start by naming one of the products from the list below. Ask the children to think of as many different ways as they can to reuse it.

- writing paper
- paper lunch bags
- cardboard boxes
- cardboard berry baskets
- cardboard egg cartons
- toilet-tissue tubes
- paper-towel tubes
- paper grocery sacks
- holiday wrapping paper

Extension: Talk about alternatives to using paper products, such as bringing your own bags to the grocery store and using cloth or metal lunch containers, cloth towels, and washable glasses and dishes.

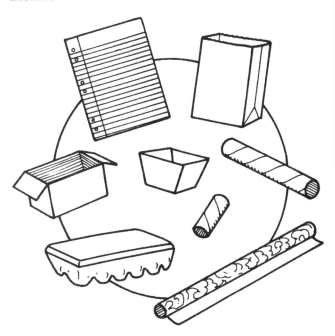

Look and Gently Touch

Explain to your children that whenever they walk through a forest, they must remember the rule, "Leave it where you find it." Picking flowers or digging up plants hurts the forest's web of life. Many forest plants produce seeds. These seeds lie dormant in the ground until the following year when they will grow into plants that will produce the next year's seeds. If the plants are removed, there will be no seeds for the following year. Take your children out on a walk to practice this rule. Encourage them to look at and gently touch the nature items they come across, but to leave them where they are.

Forest Patterns

Deciduous Tree

Forest Patterns

Evergreen Tree

Forest Patterns

Bear

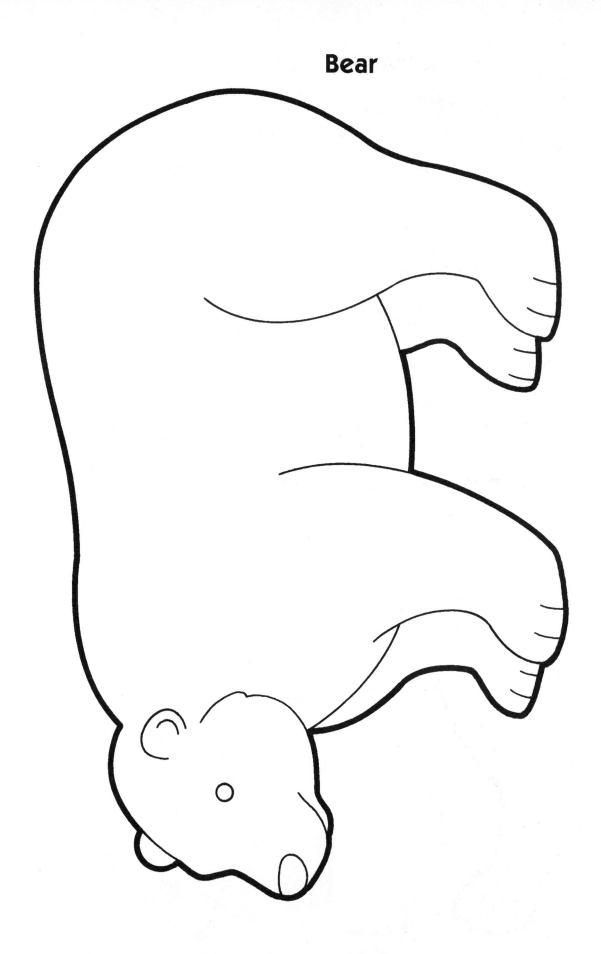

Mouse

Deer

Raccoon

Porcupine

Owl

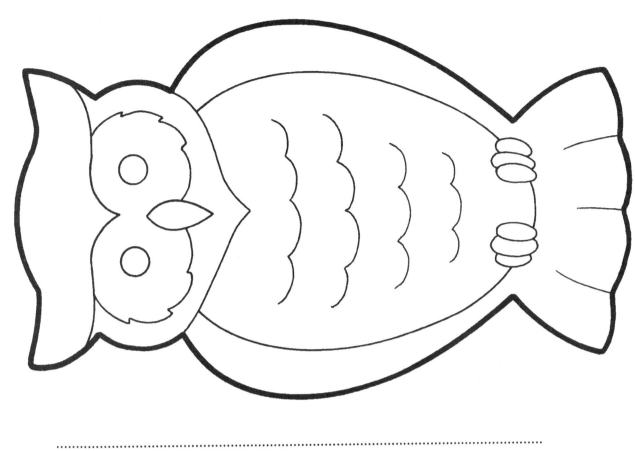

Squirrel

Forest Patterns

91

Birds

Forest Patterns

Skunk

Wolf

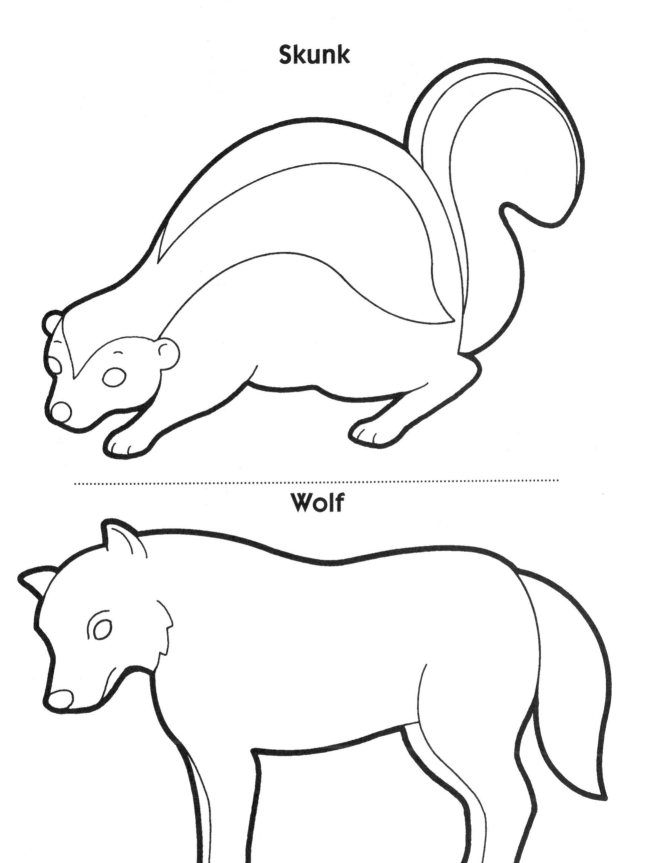

Forest Patterns

CHILDREN'S BOOKS ABOUT WOOD AND THE FOREST

FICTION

Bear, John Schoenherr, (Putnam, 1991).

Ellie the Evergreen, Jean Warren,
    (Warren Publishing House, Inc., 1993).

The First Dog, Jan Brett,
    (Harcourt Brace Jovanovich, 1992).

Hello, Tree!, Joanne Ryder, (Dutton, 1991).

In a Cabin in a Wood, Darcie McNally, (Dutton, 1991).

Just a Dream, Chris Van Allsburg,
    (Houghton Mifflin, 1990).

North Country Night, Daniel San Souci,
    (Doubleday, 1990).

Once There Was a Tree, Natalia Romanova,
    (Dial, 1989).

Owl Babies, Martin Waddell, (Candlewick Press, 1992).

Owl Moon, Jane Yolen, (Putnam, 1987).

NON-FICTION

A B Cedar: An Alphabet of Trees, George & Ella Lyon,
(Orchard, 1989).

Feathers for Lunch, Lois Ehlert,
(Harcourt Brace Jovanovich, 1990).

Forest, Ron Hirschi, (Bantam, 1991).

Red Leaf, Yellow Leaf, Lois Ehlert,
(Harcourt Brace Jovanovich, 1991).

Sleepy Bear, Lydia Dabcovich, (Dutton, 1985).

Tool Book, Gail Gibbons, (Holiday House, 1982).

The Toolbox, Anne Rockwell, (Macmillan, 1990).

Tools, Venice Shone, (Scholastic, 1991).

Children's Book List

Hands-on, creative teaching ideas from Totline® books

PIGGYBACK® SONG SERIES

Piggyback Songs

More Piggyback Songs

Piggyback Songs for Infants and Toddlers

Piggyback Songs in Praise of God

Piggyback Songs in Praise of Jesus

Holiday Piggyback Songs

Animal Piggyback Songs

Piggyback Songs for School

Piggyback Songs to Sign

1•2•3 SERIES

1•2•3 Art

1•2•3 Games

1•2•3 Colors

1•2•3 Puppets

1•2•3 Murals

1•2•3 Books

1•2•3 Reading & Writing

1•2•3 Rhymes, Stories & Songs

1•2•3 Math

1•2•3 Science

ABC SERIES

ABC Space

ABC Farm

ABC Zoo

ABC Circus

CELEBRATION SERIES

Small World Celebrations

Special Day Celebrations

Yankee Doodle Birthday Celebrations

Great Big Holiday Celebrations

CUT & TELL SERIES

Scissor Stories for Fall

Scissor Stories for Winter

Scissor Stories for Spring

TEACHING TALE SERIES

Teeny-Tiny Folktales

Short-Short Stories

Mini-Mini Musicals

THEME-A-SAURUS® SERIES

Theme-A-Saurus

Theme-A-Saurus II

Toddler Theme-A-Saurus

Alphabet Theme-A-Saurus

Nursery Rhyme Theme-A-Saurus

Storytime Theme-A-Saurus

TAKE-HOME SERIES

Alphabet & Number Rhymes

Color, Shape & Season Rhymes

Object Rhymes

Animal Rhymes

LEARNING & CARING ABOUT

Our World

Our Selves

Our Town

MIX & MATCH PATTERNS

Animal Patterns

Everyday Patterns

Holiday Patterns

Nature Patterns

EXPLORING SERIES

Exploring Sand

Exploring Water

Exploring Wood

1001 SERIES

1001 Teaching Props

1001 Teaching Tips

OTHER

Super Snacks

Celebrating Childhood

Home Activity Booklet

23 Hands-On Workshops

Cooperation Booklet

Totline books are available at school-supply stores and parent-teacher stores.

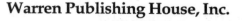

Warren Publishing House, Inc.